HAS, I AND YOU

Has, I and You

Erika Burton

CONTENTS

Dedication v

-   Guide 1
1 - Mouse, Cat and Dog 6
2 - Grace 18
3 - Carrots 30
4 - Grace's Face 42
5 - All About Dog, Cat and Mouse 54

About the Author 66

Copyright © 2025 by Erika Burton

All rights reserved. No part of this book may be reproduced in any manner whatsoever without written permission except in the case of brief quotations embodied in critical articles and reviews.

First Printing, 2025

To Anyone Who Needs to Read This--You are good enough!

Guide

I've designed this learn-to-read series to make teaching new readers simple and fun. Combining my background as a homeschooling mother with my knowledge from my Bachelor of Social Work degree, I've taken my personal experiences and mixed that with my understanding of children and the English language to create this series. Each book contains 5 short stories which cover early reading concepts, sight words and vocabulary. A few minutes of your time, your patience and love will go a long way in encouraging success with your new reader. Practicing the sight words (these are simply the common words used in the English language that either are difficult to sound out and/or are so often used that it makes sense to just have them memorized) throughout the day (make a sight word wall, play sight word games, etc) will help your new reader gain mastery over their new reading skills. The accompanying workbook (sold separately) has some helpful worksheets and sight word cut-outs as well for playing sight word games and making a sight word wall.

The purpose behind these learn-to-read books is simple and heartfelt--provide a practical and empowering resource for teaching kids to read. I get it--young kids don't usually like sitting still for long periods of time. Hence, I've curated each of the 5 short story "lessons" in this book to be completed in about 15 minutes following the method I've outlined below. My method shares with you some of the steps I have used (and use) when teaching my kids how to read and had the most success with.

My Method:

1. Pick a story and look through the pages with your child. Observe the illustrations and ask your new reader questions about what they see on the pages. Take your time.
2. Go over the sight word and vocabulary list for the book a few times. Have your child to repeat the words after you if they don't know them.
3. Read the story out loud to your new reader slowly, pointing to each word as you read.
4. Have your new reader try reading the book out loud to you with either you or your child pointing to the words. Offer hints by pointing to the drawings or asking questions and help sound out the words if they are struggling.
5. Have patience, keep practicing and happy reading! Enjoy this beautiful time you get to spend with your new reader!

Tips:
--Hints can be quite helpful. When first having your child read the stories out loud to you themselves, they will likely need some

hints. Try pointing to the drawings/part of the drawing the word they are struggling with is referring to (ex. point to the pig if the word they are to read is "pig"). If they are to read the word "like", try prompting with a question such as, "How does Cat feel about the...?" as well as helping sound out the word slowly (lllllllliiiiiii-iikk...). Sometimes, it can be helpful to have your child read the same sentence twice, especially if they needed a lot of help to read it the first time. With it fresh in their mind, they may just be able to go from hardly able to read the sentence to almost reading all the words themselves.

--When YOUR child is ready to learn to read, that is the best time to start teaching them. In other words, don't force it. Whether they are 4 or 7 years old, it doesn't really matter. What matters is that they have that supportive and encouraging person who helps them on their reading journey, whenever the time comes for that to start. If your child really has no interest, try waiting for a few weeks or even a month or two before trying again. There are lots of other ways to continue teaching some key early reading concepts in the meantime (such as reading out loud to your child) without having a formal "lesson". Relax, get creative and most importantly, have fun! If you're not enjoying the time with your child, chances are they are going to pick up on your energy and meet your lack of enthusiasm with a similar emotion.

--Get their wiggles out first. I've had much more success with my kids being able to focus on the reading lesson when they are well-fed and after they've been physically active. If they are jumping off the walls or have been sitting for a while, try ten minutes of physical activity with them (a great way for everyone to get fit!). A dance party, a workout (check out my kid-friendly workouts online), a short hike or walk around the block, a few races around the house outside or a quick obstacle course are only a few options. Get involved and join in--ten minutes goes by quickly and it's easy to get your heart rate up as well.

--Read lots to your child. Carve out time each day to read age-appropriate books with your child. Take the time to allow them to enjoy the drawings and discuss what you guys see before moving on to reading the words. Point to each word as you read and slowing read the word too. Even if it's the millionth time you've read the story, try to not rush through it. Familiar stories are often one of the best tools for teaching sight words and early reading skills because children start to pick up on the words naturally much like how they learn to comprehend spoken words and start to speak. Perhaps try playing a game with the words when you read. For instance, if your child knows the words "the" and "is", do a quick review of those two words before beginning the story and then tell them that they are going to be in charge of reading those words in the story while you read the other words. With time and practice, particularly with those old favorites, it won't be long before your child is doing most of the reading and you're the one reading the few odd words they haven't mastered (or memorized).

--Words of encouragement go a long way. Try to avoid offering meaningless praise and instead, focus on specific things you noticed (ex. "You really seem to have mastered the sight words "the" and "is"!", "Last time you really struggled with this story but today you barely needed any help at all.") .

--Don't forget--teaching your child to read can be a fun and rewarding experience! So relax, get creative and enjoy this wonderful opportunity with your child!

Dear New Reader,

    I am so excited that you are starting out on your journey to reading! I created these learn-to-read books with you in mind. It is my hope that these books help you see how fun it is to read and that you realize how capable you are of learning to read. Sometimes there will be challenging moments but I want you to know that I believe that you can learn to read. More importantly, I hope you believe you can learn to read. With practice and time, you will become a great reader!

In Gratitude,
Erika

1
MOUSE, CAT AND DOG

This is Mouse.

This is Cat.

This is Dog.

Mouse likes apples.

Mouse does not like Cat.

Mouse does not like Dog.

Dog likes Mouse.

Dog likes Cat.

Cat likes Mouse.

Cat likes Dog.

Sight Words

does
not
like
this
is
the

Vocabulary

mouse
cat
dog
apples

2
GRACE

Hi! My name is Grace.

I like cats.

21 – ERIKA BURTON

I like chickens.

I like apples.

23   –   ERIKA BURTON

I like tractors.

I like fish.

I like dogs.

I like pigs.

I like birds.

I like you.

Sight Words

I
like
you
hi
my
name
is

Vocabulary

cats
apples
dogs
tractors
birds
fish
chickens
pigs

3
CARROTS

Carrots need dirt to grow.

Carrots need the sun to grow.

Carrots need water to grow.

Carrots are orange.

Sheep like carrots.

Grace likes carrots.

37 — ERIKA BURTON

Horses like carrots.

Pigs like carrots.

39 – ERIKA BURTON

Cats do not like carrots.

Carrots, carrots, carrots!

Sight Words

likes
grow
the
to
in
need

Vocabulary

carrots
horses
sheep
pigs
Grace
dirt
cats
sun
water

4

GRACE'S FACE

ERIKA BURTON

Look at Grace's face.

Look at Grace's eyes.

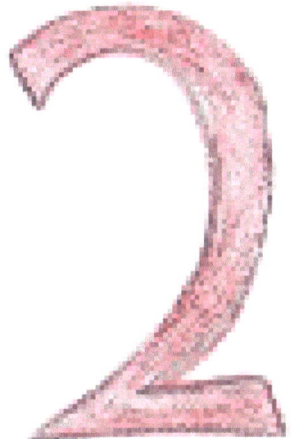

Grace has two eyes.

Look at Grace's nose.

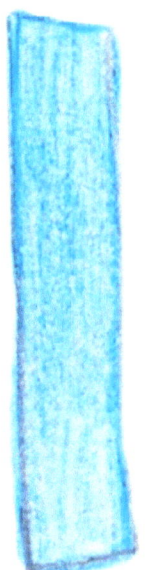

Grace has one nose.

Look at Grace's mouth.

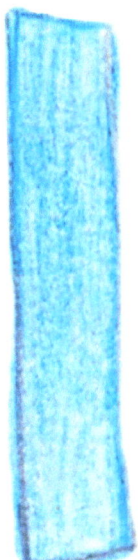

Grace has one mouth.

Look at Grace's ears.

Grace has two ears.

Sight Words

look
at
has

Vocabulary

face
eyes
nose
mouth
ears
one
two

5
ALL ABOUT DOG, CAT AND MOUSE

Dog is brown.

Cat is yellow.

Mouse is gray.

Dog digs.

Cat climbs.

Mouse steals.

Dog eats dog food.

Cat eats cat food.

Mouse eats EVERYTHING!

Sight Words

is
eats
all
about

Vocabulary

cat
dog
mouse
digs
climbs
steals
food
everything

Composite Sight Word List

look
I
at
is
has
hi
likes
my
grow
name
the
does
to
not
in
this
need
all
you
about

About the Author

Erika Burton has a Bachelor of Social Work degree and has been educating, raising and caring for children for over 20 years. She is a homeschooling mother and decided to develop these learn-to-read books to assist others in guiding kids on the reading journey. She felt that there needed to be more simple and straightforward books for learning to read after struggling with the resources available when teaching her oldest two kids to read. Her purpose for HALV ROUNDTABLE Learning is from her heart--to provide practical tools for teaching and raising holistically healthy, intelligent and empowered kids.